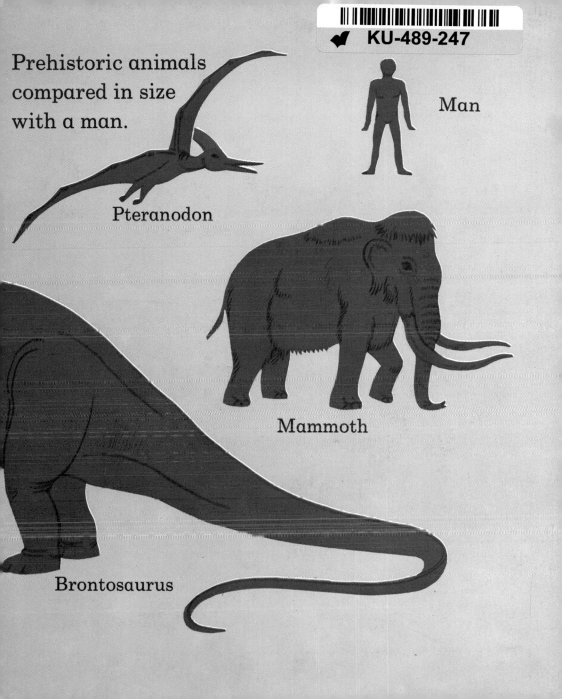

Prehistoric animals compared in size with a man.

Man

Pteranodon

Mammoth

Brontosaurus

First Published in 1970 by
Macdonald and Company
(Publishers) Limited
St. Giles House
49-50 Poland Street
London W1

Managing Editor
Michael W. Dempsey B.A.

Chief Editor
Angela Sheehan B.A.

Made and printed in Great Britain
by A. Wheaton & Company
Exeter Devon

MACDONALD FIRST LIBRARY

Prehistoric Animals

Macdonald Educational
49-50 Poland Street
London W1

Many millions of years ago, the
world was an empty place.
There were no plants.
There were no animals.
There were no people.

After a long time,
there were plants and
animals living in the
sea.
Millions of years later,
other plants and animals
lived on the land.

The pictures show some
of the animals that once
lived on the Earth.

Mammoth

Duck-billed
dinosaur

Drepanaspis

Lituites

Prehistoric animals lived on the Earth long
before there were people to write about them.

We know about prehistoric animals
because their bones were turned to stone
after they died.
These bones can now be found in rocks.
They are called fossils.

Sometimes fossil bones of a large prehistoric animal are found in rocks.
The rock is carefully chipped away from the bones.
Then the bones are put together so that people can see what the animal looked like.

skeleton of Iguanodon

Fossils of big animals are hard to find.
Fossils of small animals are found in many rocks.
Often they are shells of animals which once lived in the sea.

Ammonite fossil

5

The first animals lived in the sea.
Some were like the animals that live
in the sea today.
Jellyfish floated in the water.
Worms lived in the mud at the bottom.

There were also small animals called trilobites.
Trilobites were very strange indeed.

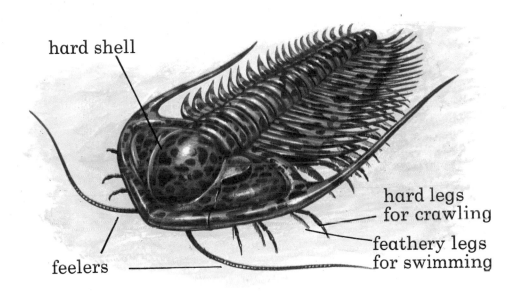

hard shell

hard legs
for crawling

feathery legs
for swimming

feelers

A trilobite had no eyes.
It used feelers to find its way about.
It lived at the bottom of the sea and dug
in the mud for its food.

When it was frightened, the trilobite
could curl up into a ball.
Most trilobites were smaller than your
thumb.

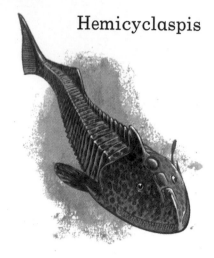

Hemicyclaspis

The first fishes had no
jaws.
Their bodies were
covered with bony
scales.
The scales protected them
like a suit of armour.

One fish was as big as
an elephant.
It had strong jaws and
ate other fish.

Dinichthys

Cladoselache

This fish was one of the first sharks.
All the bones in its body were soft.

This fish was like many
fishes which live in
the sea today.
It had hard bones.
It also had an air-bag
in its body which
helped it to float.

Cheirolepis

As time passed, less and less rain fell.
Big rivers turned into muddy pools and
many fishes died.
But some fishes could breathe out of water.
They also had strong fins which they
could use as legs.
These fishes crawled out of the water
and began to live on the land.

The fishes living on the land slowly changed.
Their legs grew stronger.
Their tails grew longer.
Their heads grew big and bony.
These were the first amphibians.
Amphibians are animals which spend most
of their life on the land.
They go back to the water to lay their eggs.

early amphibian

Eryops

Some amphibians grew very big.
Eryops was as long as a crocodile.
It had a heavy body and short, fat legs.

Eryops was a clumsy animal.
It could not run away from its enemies.
But Eryops had strong jaws to defend itself.
You can see its jaws in the fossil.

strong jaws

fossil of Eryops

12

Miobatrachus

This amphibian looked
rather like a frog.
It was called
Miobatrachus.

The largest amphibian
was bigger than a
crocodile.

Eogyrinus

It lived in swamps.
It was called Eogyrinus.

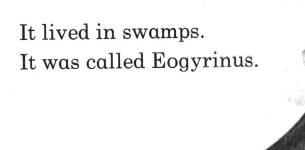

13

two of the
first reptiles

After millions of years, some amphibians
began to change.
They grew big scales on their bodies and
laid eggs with hard shells, like hens' eggs.
There was no need to lay these eggs in
the water.
They could be laid on the land.

These animals were the first reptiles.
Two of the first reptiles are shown in
the picture.

Some reptiles looked very strange.
One had a big fin on its back, like a sail.
This reptile was a meat-eater.
It ate smaller reptiles.

Dimetrodon

Some prehistoric reptiles looked like animals which live today.

Triassochelys

One looked like a turtle with a long, spiky tail.

One looked like a crocodile with a long snout.

Rutiodon

16

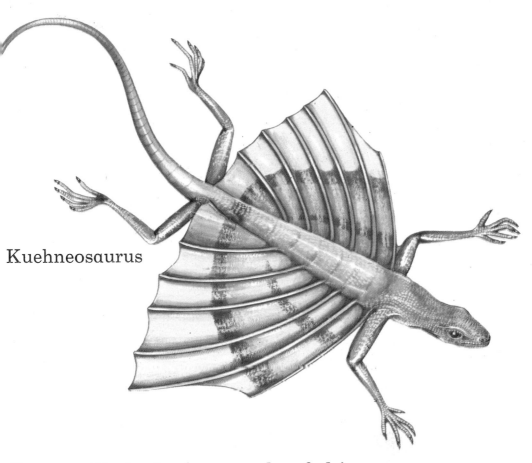

Kuehneosaurus

One reptile had wings made of skin.
This reptile did not flap its wings.
It lived in trees and glided from one
tree to another.

The biggest reptiles were the dinosaurs.
Stegosaurus was a strange dinosaur.
It had bony flaps on its back and big
spikes on its tail.
Stegosaurus looked fierce, but it ate only plants.
When it was attacked, Stegosaurus swung
its spiked tail like a club.

Stegosaurus

Brontosaurus was as big as ten elephants.
Brontosaurus was so heavy that it could
not stand for long on the land.
It spent most of the time in lakes, where
the water helped to support its body.
Brontosaurus needed so much food that it
ate plants all day long.

Brontosaurus

Many dinosaurs were peaceful plant-eaters.
Their enemies were the meat-eating dinosaurs.
The biggest meat-eater was the terrible
Tyrannosaurus.
It had huge jaws with long, jagged teeth.

Some animals could run fast enough to
escape from Tyrannosaurus.
Some had bony armour which helped to
protect them.

Triceratops

Tyrannosaurus

21

Not all the reptiles lived on the
land.
There were reptiles flying in the air and
swimming in the sea.

Flying reptiles had wings made of skin.
Some had wings bigger than any bird has
today.
They could glide over the sea for days,
looking for food.
They had long beaks.
When they saw a fish, they swooped down
and snatched it out of the water.

In the sea there were giant reptiles with
necks as long as their bodies.
Their long necks made it easy for them to
catch fish.

Pteranodon

Plesiosaurus

23

Archaeopteryx

While the great dinosaurs ruled the land,
the first bird with feathers flew in the air.
Its wings were weak and it could not fly
very well.

The first bird was called Archaeopteryx.
A fossil has been found which shows just
how this bird looked.

Archaeopteryx was the size of a crow.
It had feathers on its wings like the
birds living today.
It had teeth in its beak like the flying
reptiles which lived at that time.

fossil of Archaeopteryx

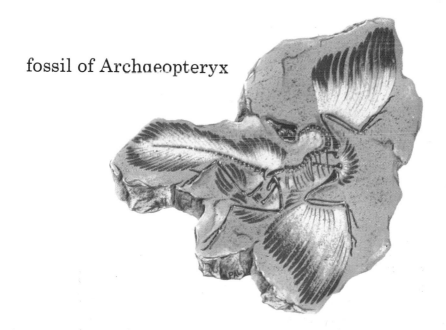

When the dinosaurs lived, there were small furry animals running about. They were so small that the dinosaurs did not bother to eat them.

The furry animals were the first mammals. They looked like rats. They ate eggs and insects.

Man

When the dinosaurs died out, mammals grew larger. There were sloths as tall as trees and pigs as big as donkeys.

Megatherium

26

The first horse had
four toes on its
front feet and three
toes on its back feet.

Eohippus

four
toes

Millions of years later,
horses had three toes on
each foot.
The middle toe was
the biggest.

Merychippus

three
toes

Today, horses have
one toe on each foot.
It is called a hoof.

modern
horse

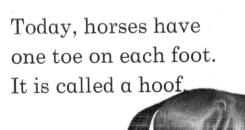

one
toe

27

About a million years ago, the world
grew very cold.
Many lands were covered with ice.

The Great Ice Age had begun.

Only animals like the mammoth were
able to live in the snow.
The mammoth had a thick, woolly coat to
keep it warm.
The other animals moved to warmer parts
of the world.

Mammoths have been found frozen in ice.
The ice has preserved them for thousands
of years.
A refrigerator preserves food in the same
way.

29

After many years, the
world grew warmer and
the ice melted.
By this time, there was
a new creature living
on the Earth.
It was man.

Man was much smaller
than many of the animals
which lived at that time.
But he was cleverer than
any of them.
He built fires to frighten
away the wild animals.
He made spears and
hunted the mammoth
for food.

The sabre-toothed tiger was an enemy of prehistoric man.
This fierce animal had teeth as big as daggers.
Man used his spears to fight the sabre-toothed tiger.
Man was so clever that he became the most important creature in the world.

Index

MACDONALD FIRST LIBRARY

Dimetrodon

Tyrannosaurus